T0193868

Life, Love and Lessons

GREGORY L. MILLER

iUniverse®

LIFE, LOVE AND LESSONS

iUniverse books may be ordered through booksellers or by contacting:

iUniverse
1663 Liberty Drive
Bloomington, IN 47403
www.iuniverse.com
1-800-Authors (1-800-288-4677)

ISBN: 978-1-5320-6900-0 (sc)
ISBN: 978-1-5320-6901-7 (e)

Library of Congress Control Number: 2019902063

Print information available on the last page.

iUniverse rev. date: 02/20/2019

Contents

Life

Love

Lessons

On The Horizon

On the horizon lye's for you
indescribable great things,
so walk a walk of faith,
and hold on to your dreams

On the horizon lye's a treasure-
one that has only your name,
so don't give up on what's important,
there's so much to be gained

On the horizon lye's a blessing-
one of the perfect type,
so remember how God loves you,
and don't give up on life

On the horizon lye's a brand new day-
one of comfort, joy and peace,
so put that white flag down
when you start feeling weak

On the horizon lye's the answer
to what's bothering your soul-
On the horizon lye's rejuvenation,
for what in life takes hurtful tolls

Each Day

Each day is an opportunity

to start all over new–

A chance for us to be redeemed

and for us to redo

Each day offers tons of hope

and promise to us all,

A chance to pick ourselves back up

from yesterday's pitfalls–

Each day is a gift from God

"Carry on" He seems to say,

because God knows we're capable

of making change Each Day

Importance of Loving Yourself

As people we love many things
our pets, our family, diamond rings-
So many things from plants to cars,
the ocean waves, the sun the stars-

Hobbies, friends, a certain song,
but love for self should be most strong
Yes! love is what we all should do,
just don't omit a love for you-

Make efforts while your time is spent
to rid your life of detriment-
And to yourself always be kind,
we all should treat ourself sometimes

And yes! it's worth it to create
your happiness for your own sake-
And then it should be like a breeze,
to love others when you're pleased

More than anything or anyone else,
as people we should love ourself;
and others will find it easier too-
to show you love, when You love You

New Memory Day

In life some dwell and waddle,
too long in the dreary past-
in things that our human emotions
just can't seem to surpass

We allow these things to haunt us
like a horrifying dream-
Immobilized by yesterday's
negative and uncomfortable things

Every day is a new beginning
full of miracles like waking up;
a chance to create new memories,
and to crawl out of yesterday's rut

Today can be new memory day,
clean out that old memory bank-
Erase and replace what's weighing you down,
with reminising of joy and thanks

Whatever happened is the pass,
as in time that has gone away-
Redecorate your outlook,
and call it New Memory Day

Never give up

It's important to never give up in life,
and to always embrace your dreams-
Always believe that with God there's a way;
no matter how hard things seem

You can persevere, stay strong,
have faith that you can win-
You have more than what it takes,
hang in there don't give in

If life was without challenges,
we would lack appreciation;
for efforts that sprout great reward
and bring sweet celebration

Keep hope healthy and alive
each tick along lifes way;
no doubt you'll find the beauty,
in each and every trying day

GOD cares much more than we know,
and wants us All yes! to believe-
that with Faith and never quiting,
there's so much we can achieve

Bright Sides

Behind the fog there is a light,
it's shining and it's shining bright-
That light shows us a brighter side,
because as people we have cried

About the things that make us sad
and things that make us oh so mad-
In every low there is a high,
behind grey clouds you'll find blue skies

Just like the stars surround the moon,
Bright sides are there to outweigh gloom
So walk along that brighter trail,
where most uncounted blessings dwell

In most cases things could be far worse,
so just look on the bright side first

Why Worry?

If it triggers mental strain-Why should you worry?
If there's nothing to be gained-
Why should you worry?

If it's making you feel worse, until depression is disbursed-
And each reminder makes it hurt-
Why should you worry?

If it's a big pain in the rear-Why should you worry?
Or brings discomfort till there's tears-
Why should you worry?

If there's nothing you can do OR if there's something you can do-
And if it's making you feel blue-
Why should you worry?

If worrying can shorten life-Why should you worry?
Or cuts your insides like a knife-
Why should you worry?

If worrying can't solve a thing, while in the midst in kinda stings-
And if it breeds nightmarish dreams-
Why should you worry?

If it's giving you gray hair-Why should you worry?
If the problem doesn't care-
Why should you worry?

If it's affecting your good health, and not offering you wealth-
Take it easy on yourself-
Why should you worry?

If it's making you lose sleep-Why should you worry?
If it's peace you really seek-
Why should you worry?

If it's causing you big stress to think about unpleasant mess-
And if you know you've done your best-
Why should you worry?

Poets

Lyrical miracles,
artists of words-
Sweet unique people
that yearn to be heard

Great beautiful minds
that bring thoughts to life-
Deep thinkers that have
a special insight

Emotion designers
of various styles-
With ways that touch hearts,
and make people smile

The height of their fame
often reached on demise-
silent souls whispering
smiles from the sky

Their stories then sealed
with a mark nicely made-
Perhaps beneath heavens trees
writing under the shade

Alive they'll remain
through each written line-
Eternally moving throughout
hearts and minds

Breathing or not
may God bless their soul-
For they grace this earth
with gifts colored gold

The Great Imagination

Imagination's are infinite,
and some are rainbow bright
A gift that gives us dreamy vision;
it decorates our inner sight

They give us wonderful ideas
torwards things we want to make,
They assist our creativity
and can open beauties' gate

A special tool for artists
and fictitious writers too,
It makes pretending fun for kids,
and can embellish what we do

They can rescue your emotions
and help you to escape-
They can help you fantasize
and successfully create

They enhance our lives in ways
that carry us away-
They're powerful and limitless
and can assist you through the day

Imaginations are a blessing,
God made us all sensations-
when He gave both me and you
The Great Imagination

Childhood and Adulthood

Nothing like childhood I must say,
not a worry or care in the world
Nothing like childhood, no bills to pay,
oh what a historical pearl

Nothing like playing all day in the sun,
or laughing all day with your friends
Nothing neater or sweeter than childhood-
at times I wish it didn't end

Yes! Adulthood is wonderful,
being able to do as I please-
without permission from anyone,
I can come and can go with the breeze

Nothing like being a grown up in life,
and having an adult's respect-
To have my own home, choose a mate of my own,
and to be independently set

When we're young, we want to be older
When we're older, we want to be young-
It's funny but that's how life is,
no matter where you're from

Be glad that your eyes keep opening;
accept the beauty in both time frames-
And like childhood and adulthood,
no two days are the same

When I'm old

I ask this question from my soul
what will life be like when old?
Will I always be ignored?
so very weak and very bored
Will I always want to cry?
because I know I'm soon to die
Will I be seen in others eyes?
or live my life unrecognized
Or will I not feel very odd?
because I know and trust in God
Smile and laugh and just because,
I'm still the soul I always was

Family

The word family carries
a great deal of weight
What does it mean?
well! the word family states

Support and togetherness,
not just being kin–
More than a simple
biological trend

Some people may think
it's just made of blood lines–
But it's a link made of love,
and warm special times

You can't measure family beauty
and through life I've discovered,
that your heart is what makes
someone sister or brother

To know you have family
is to know someone cares–
and how do they show it?
well, by just being there

Through trials that bring struggle
and sometimes even tears;
displaying friendship and love
throughout the years.

A bond that's secure
and special indeed-
Family, a very divine
healthy need

The Sweet Sound
of Peace

Yesterday I heard a sound

when two people disagreed-

They calmly discussed and worked it out-

My! how sweet the sound indeed-

They tried to work it through peace

and yes! they did succeed

I turned off my radio

and television yesterday-

I heard a sound I rarely hear,

so sweet and soothing I must say-

Quietly my nerves were calmed,

the peaceful sound enhanced day

Loudness can sprout uneasiness

and can make conflict increase-

But how sweet this sound,

this sound that I've found

How sweet the sweet Sound of Peace

Remembered

If I could be remembered in any type of way

I'd like to be remembered as a good guy as I lay

One who treated people fair and try to get along,

with all whom I encountered, when I'm reflected on

May I be a good example when you think of how I lived-

May thoughts that touch upon my life be very positive

If I could be remembered by him or her or you

may I mainly be remembered for the good I tried to do

For my willingness to share, and to support my fellow man

For how I heeded empathetically, and tried to understand

May I leave good things behind, when my human life has passed

May they see me as a Good Guy, one that didn't Finish Last

A Friend

A friend is a friend, and should be till the end,
if ever a friend they were-
The word friend is deep, and divinely a treat
because love comes from friends, him or her

Friends honor their word, won't kick you to the curb
and when borrowing will pay you back-
because you they respect, they'll try not to affect
in negative ways that cause gaps

A friend won't deceive you, and will try to believe you
no matter how strange your truth sounds-
will too show you mercy, and make you feel worthy,
when this negative world shoots you down

Friends are human not perfect, but are so much worth it;
they'll support you, with no strings attached-
They keep open minds, they're gentle and kind
meaning tender, not quick to attack

Friends are kind and forgiving, offers you better living,
while sprinkling joy on your soul-
They assist you through seasons, for sweet caring reasons-
making friendships the best stories told

True friends are God sent, so the time with them spent
is precious in valuable ways-
A friend is a friend, and should be till the end-
and a special rare blessing these days

Fruit, Fresh Air and Light

If only this world had more fruit;
the spiritually nourishing kind-
The kind of fruit that feeds our soul,
thus makes our focus more divine

If only earth had more Fresh Air
not for smog, but polluted ways-
Air that makes life more inhalable-
Air that sprouts more loving days

If only we all had more Light
to guide us coast to coast,
so every heart could better see
the things that matter most

That's what, yes! Inspires me
to write the poems I write,
through literary difference makers-
through Fruit, Fresh Air and Light

The Best of Fruit

An Apple A-day keeps the doctor away

I've heard said so many times,

but the best type of fruit though not edible

is of a much healthier kind-

Spiritual fruit is a special fruit

that helps more than the physical way-

Fruit of supernatural nutrients;

adding sweet divine strength to your day

A Story of Wisdom

There stood alone three houses
on a street named "What You Know"
and in each house lived a man-
All three were itellectuals

There was Mr. Education,
Mr. Wise, and Mr. Smart-
And all three in their own way
indeed were very sharp

So every town member gathered
to have a big debate-
To see whose mind was better
and mentally more great

First was Mr. Education
to show what he could do-
He displayed his super knowledge,
from countless books that he read through

All the people in that town
were very much impressed-
He seemed equipped for any job,
or any written test

Next was Mr. Smart who had
for sure the quickest mind-
He displayed fast problem solving,
and did so in record time

Everyone in town again
were very much impressed-
He could fix or figure out anything-
Oh what a great clever mind he possessed

Then last was Mr. Wise,
and great Life Lessons he did bring
He lectured them on peace, good health
and finding joy in simple things

He spoke of good decision making;
common sense, and yes! The Lord
He left them all in awe-
And oh so pleasingly floored

Mr. Wise was the best, and did more than impress-
He was much more than book smart, or clever-
He opened their eyes, taught them how to be wise-
Through lessons they kept yes! Forever

Rich at Heart

When you own a rich heart,
you own a great treasure-
When you own a rich heart,
you bring others pleasure

A heart full of love
is worth more than gold-
Rich hearts can add
great warmth to your soul

When you own a rich heart
you're a joyous success,
and little everyday things
suddenly are the best

Rich hearts are full
so they need not depend,
on material things
and how much they spend

When you own a rich heart
you stand silently tall-
Because love outweighs everything,
money and all

Yet So Much Alike

We're all so very different

yet all so much alike-

We all eat to stay alive

and we all have trials in life-

We're all so very different

yet similar indeed-

Our late parents are the same

father Adam, mother Eve-

We're all so very different

yet I see you in me-

You send peculiar vibes

that I relate to innerly-

We're all so very different

but yes! the bottom line,

is that we're all flesh, blood, and spirit-

with unique God given minds

A Child

A child has beauty to behold,

and immeasurable worth

A child is like a piece of gold,

that decorates this earth

A child is a precious treasure,

that trumps every adjective

A child can keep you rich inside,

and make life wonderful to live

A Sweeter Wine

I'm just a little older,
I'm just a sweeter wine-
Not too many come this far
without a wiser mind

I'm still good as gold,
with silver in my hair-
wrinkles, maybe one or two,
yet smiles are never rare

How about some conversation?
my stories you might like;
stories based on roads I've crossed,
and things I've done in life

I'm just a little slower,
not quite fast as most-
just aging rather gracefully,
with father time I coast

Not too many come this far
without a wiser mind-
I'm just a little older,
I'm just a sweeter wine

The Patient Man

The patient man was always calm
and never in a hurry-
He knew how to take his time,
which helped him not to worry

No problem for the patient man
to wait in any line
He knew how to pace himself
along with father time

He never stared at clocks,
nor did he pace the floor-
He twiddled not a finger
when time was passing more

He didn't quickly anger
when things were going wrong-
He rolled with life's best punches
when tough days came along

If there was anything he wanted,
he'd disregard the length of time,
and work until he got it,
so worth it in his mind

He always kept a special cool,
and stayed calm as any lake-
was wise, and learned in life
that good can come to those who wait

Seasons

There's seasons for the holidays,
and nature's seasons too
There's pleasant happy seasons,
and seasons sad and blue

There's seasons for both life and death
and even for sports fans-
There's seasons when we must adjust,
yes! seasons for new plans

I've watched them come and watched them go
these periods of change-
I've watched them long enough to know
that nothing stays the same

The reasons for the seasons
are not that very odd-
The reasons for the seasons
are to learn and notice God

Accept each and every season;
go with each seasons' flow-
Seasons teach us how to live
and help us all to grow

Stars

Mysterious ornaments towering high-

Lucky emblems of space decorating the sky

Scattered romance, sweet magical sight-

they lurk over earth as if guarding the night

Sprinkled bright silver that twinkles at times-

as if heaven's lights, a great Godly shine

Wonderous beauty, miraculous art;

tone setter for lovers invading the dark

Everything has a purpose and so does a star-

They're made to admire, and lovely they are

Dreaming

It's okay to dream,
it's a beautiful thing-
Dreams can inspire,
bring high powered desire-
Dreams can ignite realitys' fire

It's okay to dream
though far-fetched some may seem;
because dreams install magic
that allow you to have it,
and can help you accomplish great things

Yes! so many people
that were surely your equal,
rode the wings of their dreams to their goal-
so may your life include dreaming,
with zealous eye's beaming-
while you march till one day it unfolds

My Poetry my Friend

I have a friend inside of me,
that brings comfort to my soul-
One that offers therapy,
and tops the finest gold

One that welcomes my opinion
and always lends an ear,
one that helps me be creative-
one that's so divine and dear

Yes! one that shares my view
and also entertains-
one that's unconditional,
and helps to ease life's pain

God has blessed me with a partner
that will be there till the end,
and I'm forever grateful-
my poetry and friend

The Beauty Of Rain

Happy tears of the sky,

cooling the day-

Nature's best friend

live without it? No way!

Can you see the beauty

or do you see gloom?

Much more than the sun,

the rain beautifies June-

So never let rain

be an unwelcomed sight,

because rain is the hero

of everyone's life-

It might come with thunder

and lightning at times,

or might postpone a trip

that you planned in your mind

But it's Gods' special potion,

like sprinkles of love-

so whenever it rains

just be happy it does

It just takes one sentence

in fact to explain-

The beauty of life,

is the Beauty of Rain

The Trees

When I look upon the trees
in me they form a smile-
Indescribably exquisite,
and full of lovely style

When I look upon the trees
a peacefulness I find within me-
The rest of nature looking up
at trees with quiet envy

I think about if trees could hug,
I'm sure the best hug it would be-
What could be a better sight
than the beauty of a tree

They live and breathe like you and me,
while moving ever slow;
only bulging for the wind,
or when it's time to grow

For many forms of life
trees offer homes and safe escapes
And like a friend to everyone,
great breathing air they make

When I look upon the trees
I'm glad for fruit and wood
When I look upon the trees,
I see a lot of Godly good

It's Summertime

Once again it's summertime,
sweet smiling yellow sun-
Kids in a festive frenzy
as they bask in summer fun

The flowers trees and grass
are a lovely summer's hue-
The skies are bright and pretty
so the birds are happy too

Aroma from an outdoor grill
to blend with summers air-
Boaters, fishermen and swimmers,
are splashing here and there

A season when we slap at bugs
because they're always bugging-
Folks are laid out on the beach,
in parks love birds are loving

Ball fans are at the stadium
to watch their teams at bat,
and bones that ached from winter chill
are now soothed and relaxed

Yes! once again it's summertime
so get your summer gear
And say goodbye to all the cold,
for summertime is here

Snow

Snow so pretty - Snow so cold

twisting, turning

as it flows

A floating cotton in the air,

and not a single

matching pair

Winter dust undressing trees,

as it forces

falling leaves

Some might smile, and some might frown

as each white flake

clings to the ground

And too for some fun by the load

Snow so pretty - Snow so cold

Thanks 2 Appreciate You

Thank you for your love;
the love you show each day
For being kind and so considerate-
For making sure that I'm okay

For doing all the little things
that mean so very much;
things that go beyond the surface
and that make life not so rough

It truly is a blessing
having someone such as you;
you offer me the great support
which helps me make it through

So very rare it is these days
to find nice people in your life-
One's that offer patience;
the unselfish caring type

I know these are only words,
but you're all these words times ten
Thanks for being so lovingly special-
Thank you my lover and friend

Your Smile

Your smile is like a lucky charm,

and brighter than a star

Your smile could win a trillion hearts,

so beautiful by far

If you were into showbiz

your smile would draw great crowds-

And if applied on rainy days

I'm sure would clear the clouds-

And for someone who could not see

I'm sure your smile would touch-

it's pleasantly attractive

and I love it very much

Always making someone's day

and could tame a crocodile-

Worth much more than words can say

is your big pretty smile

As New Love Begins

The fortunate fingers of the wind
giddily caressed her hair through;
the breeze biasly fondled my mind-
thus creating a heart yearning view

Peripheral vision escaped in an instant,
erasing all but what my soul embraced-
the sun then pursued beholding her,
shimmering down on its prize, her sweet face

My vision became one with my hearing,
seeing sound in lovely prism-
Oh to view this symphony of beauty-
shape orchestrated, colorful rhythm

A living doll, a breathing angel-
A visual massage, filled with enamoring power
My eyes charasmatically danced on her posture-
adrenaline ascending to heights of towers

The air of the universe befriended me;
favorably whispering to her what I felt-
directing her eyes to my deep admiration,
as our eyes touched we made climates melt

In her consciousness seeped the great energy
of my then serendipitous heart-
Her reciprocal awareness beamed my way,
obliging our dreamy new start

Sweet And Simple

Sweet and simple
my love for you-
always fresh
and always new

Pleasant as
a peace of mind-
comforting as
springs sunshine

More beautiful
than any song-
and guaranteed
forever long

More than a poets
words can say-
Love reaching out
when you're away

A friendly love
that's warming too
My Sweet and Simple
Love For You

Time's Test

Each relationship is tested
by what we know as time-
Time reveals unknowns
and shows us many signs

Times test can be difficult,
some fail and some do pass-
It takes wisdom, love and chemistry
for most relationships to last

Times test requires patience,
respect and good communication-
And of course unselfishness,
for love to be a time sensation

But you can't just have one artist
for love to be a masterpiece-
It takes two to shape and form a love;
one that stays healthy, strong and sweet

Times test can be quite a haul;
you will encounter stormy weather,
but often worth it if you stick it out-
Pray for each other and together

Remaining Views of You

One day when you're old

and mirrors paint a wrinkled you-

What you have inside

will keep your beauty shining through

One day when you're old

and your body starts to slow-

what you have inside

will make up for what's physical

One day when you're old

and your days on earth are few-

what you have inside

will keep you wonderful and new

So one day when you're old

you need not be sad or ashamed-

because what you have inside

will make my view of you the same

Even Though

There's something you must
always know-
and that is
I love you even though

Though we have
our ups and downs-
though at times
you make me frown
I love you even though

Though sometimes
you make me rant-
or answer no,
and say you can't
I love you even though

Though you sometimes
trigger irks
through things that
even sometimes hurt
I love you even though

Though you're not perfect
many days
you warm my heart
with sweet sun rays
I love you even though

These words I say here
barely show,
the expert way
I love you so

Love shows its
meaning like a pro-
when love is love,
through Even Though

Empathy and Symphathy

I emphasis my empathy,

when it comes to you and me-

your qualms become my melody,

you're looked upon essentially

And I utilize my sympathy,

through a caring symphony-

I do so instrumentally-

You mean a lot to God through me

Should life tie you in troubled knots,

both forms of love from me you got-

yes! as in empathy sympathy dock-

You mean an empathy sympathy lot

Thank You for Being Likable

I know love is powerful,
and the greatest in the end-
but thank you for being likable,
for ways that spell great friend

I'm sure I'll always love you
but what makes you so great;
is an ingredient called likable-
awesome icing on loves cake

The smiles and laughter that you offer;
the joyous comfort that you bring,
makes you oh so very likable
and helps me get through prickly things

Thank you for being likable-
it so helps our love to work
I love you deeply, but I like you too-
Oh what a blessing of a perk

Take Your Time

You don't want to rush love-
You gotta take your time,
and never look too hard
if it's love you want to find

Get an understanding;
show patience from the start-
Get to know the one you're loving
to prevent a broken heart

And don't let physical desires
erase what could have been-
Learn to love their heart and mind,
that's the only way to win

Search the heart of whom
you choose to be your loving mate;
they're not worthy of your love
if their character is fake

If it's meant for you to have someone,
God's light on you will shine-
If it was or wasn't meant to be
you'll know, so take your time

You Can Love Again

Never toss a heart aside
yes! I mean the one in you-
Never just throw love away
no matter what you do

You have a heart inside you,
one made to love, and love again-
a heart that's stronger than you think,
one that knows love has no end

Never just throw love away
and never throw away your life-
Love is what we're all about,
let love remain your guiding light

I know heart breaks are painful
and can hurt so deep within;
if you were able to love once,
you can love and love again

Acts of Love

When some relationships are lacking
in areas of wants and needs,
it could be the lack of acts of love-
acts of love plant healthy seeds

There's so many opportunities
to do kind deeds everyday;
so many easy little things,
that help folks on their loving way

Just offering a simple beverage
or perhaps help with a chore;
sharing tastey food,
or maybe opening a door

Just asking how are you?
or subtle compliments go far-
Don't take loving time for granted,
work to keep love up to par

Easy common knowledge things,
take love further than some think-
yes! further than material;
acts of love can smooth out kinks

Be considerate and show them
that it's them you're thinking of,
by doing little tid bits daily
that are known as acts of love

Let Love Be Love

How can love be defined,
or ever be worth it;
If love can't be love
when things are not perfect

Give love room to breath,
let love be itself-
let love keep it's wings
and always be felt

Let love do what it should,
through every trial-
that's when love can be love,
and stay love all the while

And when love is love
it's much more than worth it-
it's strength and beauty revealed,
when situations aren't perfect

How Beautiful
Life Can Be

Oh how beautiful
life can be,
when everyone's living
in harmony

With effort applied
torwards getting along;
with prioritized patience-
when compassion is strong

Oh how beautiful
to climb out of bed,
knowing folks aren't against you,
or after your head

When people add comfort
through welcoming smiles;
without favoritism,
but with all for one styles

Oh how beautiful
life can be-
when you know I love you,
and I know you love me

Talk To Me

Talk to me, make me aware,

of what goes on because I care

Talk to me, don't keep away,

what I should know about your day

Communicate my mate and friend-

Don't separate us now and then;

nor be selfish with your thoughts-

All verbal silence we must halt

Don't deprive our understanding,

or our rapport won't be expanding

We'll never grow and sink so low,

so Talk To Me, so I can know

Keep the Light On

Love has a way of changing
darkness into Light-
Love is life's top and bottom line-
so keep the Light on day and night

The Light isn't electric or even solar ran,
and shines brighter than yes the sun-
It has a switch that's in the heart
of each and everyone

Keep the Light on in your home, at work,
in every atmosphere or place-
This Light is very affordable,
but light we can't afford to waste

Keep your Light switch upwards
and upwards you'll ascend-
Shine your Light for all to see;
with the Light On we all win

Love Is A Choice

When you put it in your mind
to take care of anything-
You've made a choice to love;
caring is what loving means

And yes! it's just that simple
simple as choosing to care
Showing care defines you love;
don't leave loves cubbard bare

We're all capable of loving
because we're capable of choice-
It's using our free will;
please heed my loving voice

Use your own free will
to care for human beings-
Fill your will with love;
turn this planet's pastures green

Love is more than just emotion,
keep your heart willingly awake-
Make the choice to love today,
for mankind and goodness sake

Conditional and Unconditional Love

When people love you only
for how you make them feel,
that's a form of conditional love,
and is questionably real

When you're loving someone solely
for what they have to offer you-
that's also a conditional love;
a selfish way of loving too

When you stop doing someone favors
and then barely see their face-
that too could be conditional love-
one that's not at all so great

But when you love someone for them,
not just for you, and all they do;
that's an unconditional love-
love that's profound and true

Not just in mate relationships
but in any other type-
true love is when you love someone
with selfless ways in sight

Whether family, neighbor, mate
or someone from around the way-
you know you're loved unconditionally,
when they love you come what may

A Great Opportunity

There's a wonderful opportunity-
one waiting just for you;
Something that helps everyone
and what we all should do

We all should take advantage
of this chance to do one thing-
one that covers all the bases-
one that takes away life's stings

An opportunity that fits our hearts
just like a perfect glove;
life's greatest opportunity-
Take time today to love

Loves Gang

Love is my name,
you can join my gang,
if along with me you could-
whether guy or girl, add to better this world,
then together we'll make earth good

"Ok! well I'm Mr. Peace-
I put minds at ease,
my gentle ways are enough to adore"
Yes! Join me Peace if you will-
fewer folks will be killed,
and you'll help folks relax, come aboard

"Hello! I'm Dr. Compassion-
I apply tender fashion
that helps those with misfortune out"
Great with you I relate, you'll help defeat hate,
come along, your warm ways carry clout

"Well, My name is Forgiving
and I add to living
by showing folks merciful ways"
Yes! come your my type, many tears you'll help wipe,
you're supernaturally healthy these days

Greetings! I'm Mrs. Deeds
and I give those in need-
my labor, my time and kind gifts"
Your resume's great, you have what it takes;
through generous ways that uplift

Yes more peace we need,
compassion and deeds,
and hearts that forgive are great
This world is so torn, do you have something warm?
that might make Earth a better place?

If you can say yes!
we can all pass a test,
that we've struggled to pass for so long-
because love is the key, do your part and you'll see
the most powerful gang ever known

Why Put It Off

Why put off until tomorrow
what can be done today?
Time is very valuable-
To waste time doesn't pay

Why make a plan and cancel it?
Why let it sit and wait?
Strive to make the most of life-
Why procrastinate?

Yesterday you can't regain,
and tomorrow's not guaranteed
Assertively improve your life-
Do yourself a deed

Whether it's constructive
or things you like to do-
Make the most of everyday;
yes! Make the most of you

So one day in the future
when you're old and grey-
You'll be glad you took the time to do
the things you did Today

Going Out And Getting Out

Yeah it's nice to see the world
and to travel to and fro,
but it can spread your home life thin
when it's frequently you go

It may be okay to visit bars
and sip from time to time,
but regret can form when you're around
so many altered minds

It's good to get out now and then
and offer's therapeutic change,
but don't sacrifice your peace
just to add more fun and games

There's nothing wrong with going places,
sometimes it's healthy and necessary-
but when you're spending too much cash
it can make bill paying scary

To take a flight, train ride or cruise
can bring great jubilation,
but the more that you're exposed to
sometimes trigger more temptation

Sometimes what we call good living
can take us out of Godly touch-
Life is to be lived,
but don't try to do too much

Going out and getting out
has turned lives a dreadful hue-
Going out and getting out is fine,
but always think it through

What is happiness?

Are you a happy person?
How is your time spent?
Do you wear a natural smile?
Are you at all content?

We all have our definition
of what happiness can be-
What's happiness to you
doesn't have to be for me

Happiness is an emotion
that comes in many shades
Happiness is priceless-
and something people rarely trade

Some may say it's having money,
but happiness sprouts from within
Happiness is a state of mind,
and can sometimes come from friends

Happiness is finding joy
and doing things you like;
a life that offers laughter,
and that offers you delight

Happiness is finding goodness
in your heart along the lifes way,
and learning to appreciate-
all that God has sent your way

The Way You Like

Treat people with kindness,
and treat people fair-
Show people patience,
and show them you care

Treat people with love,
and in ways that are equal
Greet people with smiles-
Be good to all people

Show people compassion,
and apply some respect-
torwards people you know
or the one's you just met

What I'm hoping you do-
and I'll be glad to repeat it,
is simply treat people the way
you'd like to be treated

Driving

Why is it that some never think

or hesitate to drive and drink;

unsteady so they tend to swerve-

blood stains left upon the curb

Kids left without a mom or dad

because someone went speeding mad

Go-carts and bumper cars are fun,

but cars are deadly, they weigh tons

Don't endanger other lives-

Always be careful when you drive

If you don't drink, always still say

"I'm gonna take my time today"

Because a Car is not a Toy,

but a convenience to enjoy

Be A Difference Maker

Be a difference maker-

make Earth a better place,

sprinkle love on someone's life,

enhance the human race

Be a difference maker-

by being pleasant as can be,

show the type of understanding

that increases harmony

Be a difference maker-

this world is bad enough,

be patient with your fellow man,

be gentle not so rough

Be a difference maker-

show politeness in your tone,

do tid bits that sprout joy;

forgive, and try to get along

Be a difference maker-

help lift spirits that are down,

be fair and very honest

as you walk about your town

Be a difference maker-

and if you just do your part;

maybe other folks will notice-

thus triggering more caring hearts

Looking for Happiness

An unhappy man, formulated a plan
to find happiness, and searched-
He tried changing friend's, but still no happy grin-
but put his plan right back to work

He bought a new car, sharp and fit for a star,
which he drove, and did get a few thrills-
yet something still missing, and time was still ticking-
His happiness still unfulfilled

Determined he was, and it was because
he wasn't the type to give up;
thought he might be set, if he purchased a pet-
still unhappy, though with a nice pup

Frustrated no doubt, with hope running out-
He too even changed his spouse,
which was extreme, his new spouse turned out mean,
so he thought "I'll just buy a new house"

Though he liked his home, there were still empty moans
and it took him a few years to find-
that it didn't take change, it just took a brain-
learning happiness came from his mind

Happy he was, and happy he stayed
as he laughed at himself looking back;
at that unhappy man, with such all for not plans-
thinking wow it was easy as that

Temples

Our body is our temple
made of many precious parts,
so treat it like a treasure
and especially your heart

Our body is a toolbox
so keep up with your tools-
By keeping healthy habits
and not being drug abused

Nothing of material
could be of greater worth-
Healthy bodies are imperative,
while we're here on earth

Respect and take care of your body-
Healthy bodies help our mind,
and when our bodies are in shape
it helps us smile more time to time

Healthy bodies are important
it's just that plain and simple;
it's a gift that you should cherish-
for yes! it is your TEMPLE

Let it go

When people trouble you in life
there's something you should know,
which is it's very crucial
that we learn to let it go

When people disrespect you
and bring discomfort to your life,
don't be marred internally-
Nor feel you always have to fight

Don't let your joy be stolen
or let your peace forever wane-
Nor let your emotions
trigger deep regret or shame

You help yourself immensely
when you ignore bad spirits-
It's wise to let go of a problem,
and it doesn't mean you fear it

You need not stoop that low-
Like a river let it flow,
learn from your experience,
and simply let it go

Our Co-workers

Our Co-workers are family

in an inevitable way-

that's why it's so important

that we get along each day

Sometimes we spend more time with them

than our family at home-

so do your part, loan out your heart

and treat them like your own

Let love decorate your atmosphere,

so you don't have a job you dread-

because love and laughter makes it easier

to work and leave your bed

We Should all be Healthy and Happy

If you owned a fancy car
would you be happy then?
If you had a snazzy wardrobe
would you keep a happy grin?

Would a bunch of money
make you happy through and through?
Or a big house and a boat
would that make a happy you?

If you could eat and drink
the things you wanted everyday-
Would that make this world for you
a better place to stay?

Or could you still be happy
if you drove an average car?
A car that no one envies-
yet still would get you far

Could you still be happy
with a wardrobe that is fair?
With clothing warm and suitable,
but that wouldn't make folks stare

A home that has enough space
just to unwind and relax,
and shelter you from harm;
with everything in tact

And not a lot of money
but enough to pay the bills-
enough to live a healthy life,
and eat a balanced meal

Not enough to buy big fancy boats
or things that are exotic-
Not enough to make life seem unfair
or to flaunt because you got it

If just enough could make you happy
no one would be deprived,
and Earth would be a better place
for everyone alive

Mankind has every resource
that we'll ever need-
for all to be healthy and happy,
if we just eased up off the greed

Compassion

When people make mistakes some say
"that was very dumb of you",
then there's those that care enough to help
and see what they can do

When folks are feeling down some say
"That's their problem, no not mine",
then there's those that care enough
to assist folks every time

When addictions trouble folks some say
"That's their fault for being weak",
then those care enough to help
or pray them to their feet

We increase the coldness in this world
when we treat folks in any fashion-
We need more difference makers
with divineness called compassion

It's an ingredient of love,
so show support when someone falls-
There's beauty in compassion
and it's answering God's call

Because love is yes! the main thing
that our Lord wants us to do-
Open up your heart,
treat people like another you

We were put on earth together
to be there for one another-
Not to tear down, but to strengthen
and encourage our sisters and brothers

Whenever you see someone down,
don't treat them in an ugly fashion-
because we're all down time to time
and need our fellowman's compassion

The Best Example

The best examples ever

are ones that are lived not heard-

The ones in live and living color;

that tells the truth better than words

Examples that have messages

supported with representation,

makes it easier to abide by,

and with far less hesitation

So while you talk to make your point,

show your example too-

It makes it more authentic,

thus easier for them to do

You'll be a healthier role model

with silent cheers of rah rah rah-

With more respect, because your living it,

without folks hearing blah! blah! blah!

Material Gains

Oh the euphoria of material gain,

how it takes our mind high heights-

Things to touch, see and feel

are such a welcomed sight-

But they can often make us

lose sight of what matters most,

which is caring about others,

which means more than to have or to boast

Some material things are necessities

and it's ok to like this and that;

be wise by not going overboard-

it can form an uncomfortable trap

Try not to be too anxious

for what has driven some insane-

Learn to find contentment in life-

A Peace of mind offers greater gain

It's How You View Yourself

It's not how others view you,

it's how you view yourself-

Opinions always vary

so don't let them all be felt

Be comfortable with who you are,

you have your own design-

it's how you view yourself that counts,

pay negative no mind

It's how you view yourself that counts-

self motivating cheers;

most crucial fan? the inner man!

with independent ears

Other views may sometimes help,

but some unfair and mean-

that's why your own view is crucial-

keep your self-esteem

Don't worry what folks say or think,

nor feel ashamed or odd;

its views from you that really matter,

and foremost views from God

Strings

Everything has strings attached,

and domino affects-

What goes around shall come around,

that's if it hasn't came back yet

Remember everything you do

has consequences that pertains,

yes! to every situation-

that so often boomerang

So don't take anything for granted;

make prudent choices on your way-

Sew good seeds and do good deeds,

through love and wisdom everyday

The working atmosphere

The people make the difference
in most working atmospheres-
the difference in one's happiness
while working there or here

Good communication
kindness and respect-
Those three can make a difference
in production you can bet

They can also make a difference
towards climbing out of bed;
when you like the people
it's much easier instead

Showing fellow workers patience-
not being harsh or mean,
not showing favoritism,
but showing that you're all a team

Open hearted folks
that care enough to lend an ear-
can make a healthy difference
in any working atmosphere

Exercise

To exercise is very wise

and is a special key-

towards how we feel each day,

and sweet longevity

Rather walking, jogging, bikes,

aerobics or with weights-

it makes a healthy difference

and does your mind and body great

So include a little exercise

throughout your life and find,

that you'll look and feel much better-

with energy that helps you shine

To exercise is very wise

and has ingredients you need;

to live a life of quality,

and to help you to succeed

To Get An Education

An education helps you
in oh so many ways
Although it's sometimes tedious;
it helps in every phase

It not only makes us smarter
but it helps us stay alive-
A platform towards getting jobs,
so we can eat, buy homes and drive

An education helps us too
with our communication,
through understanding to expand on-
thus sprouting better conversations

It can be a mental grind,
and tedious no doubt-
Just remember when you graduate,
you'll have rewarding clout

Gaining knowledge can equip you,
and make you a future sensation-
For financial peace and strength,
it helps to get an education

Never Back Down?

Some may say that it's never okay
to back when someone provokes-
Some say "Don't be a punk-why take that junk?"
If you take crap, respect they'll demote

It doesn't mean you can't fight,
when you're mentally bright;
bright enough to realize that it's smart-
SOMETIMES smart to back down
when bad news comes around,
showing strength through a wise humble heart

Emotions sometimes put us deep
in an ocean that's hard to swim out-
That's why I say that the cool peaceful way
can be better, regardless of clout

Though others might scoff, about you being soft
The Lord will smile on you indeed-
thus evading a cell or something like hell-
that's why patience is what we all need

Remember this rhyme the very next time
your provoked by a wild angry clown-
If you have to stand STAND, but you're no less a man
if you stay in control and back down
Blessed are the peace makers,
don't be the bait taker
Those with quick tempers are flawed-
In God's word abide, be careful with pride-
Pride comes before so many fall

Just Be Yourself

Remember you're original
so always be yourself-
You're who you are for a reason-
You're unlike anyone else

Be yourself wherever you go-
Share the uniqueness of your mind,
because we're all individuals,
and undoubtedly one of a kind

Make decisions that are suitable-
to what you feel is right;
do things that apply to you-
Keep the inner you in sight

People might see you as odd
or talk about you till they're gray,
but don't alter who you are;
relax and be yourself each day

No matter what size, color, race,
background or whatever;
your personality is yours-
Our styles are rainbow like together

Physicality

Too many emphasis these days
are placed on physicality-
Unfortunately for us all
that's just reality

Physicality can often make us
all too quick to judge-
Thus judging folks unjustly,
causing strife is what it does

So often physical appearance
attract mate seekers more,
instead of looking at the heart,
which is a higher score

Athletics and anatomy-
how bodies look and what they do,
can awe minds to great degrees
and make us make poor choices too

Physical colors, shapes and sizes
becomes our focus and mindset-
even hair or one's apparall
have over emphasized affects

I wrote this poem for those
that mainly keep a surface view-
So live a life of substance,
meaning like you have a clue

Because bodies come and bodies go
but in the very end-
These bodies won't mean anything,
as dust replaces bone and skin

While a body is a blessing
of a tool to have on earth-
what they can do and how they look,
could never garner our true worth

We need to all get in the habit
of prioritizing souls,
by loving one another inwardly;
with heaven being our long term goal

A hard load to carry

A grudge is a hard load to carry,
and can surely weigh you down-
It ages you, and triggers stress,
and forms depleting inner frowns

A grudge is an ugly burden,
but a choice that's made by you;
one that can drain you spiritually,
and can stunt your progress too

A grudge is unwise and unhealthy,
and shows a lack of faith-
It's doubting what the Lord can do,
and the changes He can make

A grudge can be based on emotions,
or sometimes stubborn pride-
A grudge can rid you of your joy,
and cripple your insides

Don't be self defeated,
give peace to yourself and let go-
A grudge is a hard load to carry-
Don't comply with that evil low blow

Love yourself enough to release it,
you can let go and still not indulge-
Heavier than life's largest boulder,
is the weight of a big ugly grudge

Life Despite

Despite cold negative people,
and those that are but scoffers-
I really love and enjoy life,
and what it has to offer

I treasure and I like my life-
Life keeps me fascinated;
though my life is full of flaws
and is often complicated

Life is very special,
and it's challenges are great-
regardless of it's lows
and it's unfortunate bad breaks

I love nature and it's beauty-
I loves life's natural highs-
Life no doubt is wonderful,
although life has its' knotted ties

Though life can be a struggle
and some days can be a fight-
I love my special blessing;
the one that we call Life

Adversity University

If life ever was a college,
the perfect name would be
Adversity University-
life's description A to Z

Life is truly like a college;
without summer or spring break-
In fact no breaks at all,
and tests that start when you awake

You never know how hard a test,
or what life's school has in store-
Sometimes the tests are grueling too,
and ones that you can't study for

Any day could be a final-
our final exam so remember,
to keep your mind and spirit ready,
each day through December.

Each day expect tough challenges,
as we all just do our best-
at "Adversity University"
life in a nutshell, "Trials called Tests"

Even As

Even as we speak about
things harmful to our mind-
Something beautiful is taking place,
so lovely and sublime

Even as we live lifestyles
that diminish our own peace-
Something beautiful is taking place
so lovely and so sweet

Even as we're having fun
through choices that affect our soul-
Something beautiful is taking place,
so great and worthy to behold

Even as we watch the news,
and things that drain our spirits dry-
Something beautiful is taking place-
so atleast open one eye

And remember while you go through life,
that if you look, there's so much more-
which tells the story of lifes' beauty
and with divineness to adore

Thrill Seekers and Peace Keepers

In life there's many thrills to take
our flesh and mind high heights,
often these things take our peace-
a huge unworthy sacrifice

I must it admit it thrills me,
just keeping inner peace;
some may not understand it,
or think I've settled for the least

Some may find peace seeking boring,
in peaceful shoes they choose not be-
Thrill seekers sometimes end up groaning,
thinking oh! why me? why me?

Those that seek peace first,
seek lifes' healthy and best way-
God so wants us to have peace
and find contentment in our day

Thrill Seekers and Peace Keepers-
A bit of both may sound just fine,
but sometimes thrills can trigger chills,
that mar your soul and peace of mind

I'm not saying life should never
have great fun or things that thrill-
I'm just saying "Seek Peace First",
so you don't pay regretful bills

The Bigger Your Goals

The bigger your goals, the better your goals
and further you'll ascend-
Set your goals high as the clouds,
and you'll go much further then

Accept life's greatest challenges
and surely you will find-
That you'll bring out the best in you
yes! each and every time

Have faith that you can do
what other's have before-
Set the bar ambitiously high
and you'll accomplish more

Don't let negative opinions
stall you from endeavors-
Believe in your ability;
don't be fearful of trying whatever

Set your dreams high as a star,
you'll have a higher percentage win
The bigger your goals, the better your goals-
and further you'll ascend

First Take Care Of Home

Home is where our day begins,
it starts at home in life-
So much is offered outside home,
but first make sure home is right

Always keep your home in order,
invest in each relationship-
because home is where we lay our heads,
so make sure peace is part of it

Make sure your home is kept together
from ceiling, wall to floor,
and always make sure love
highlights its' decore

Be it family, bills or fixing things,
let healthy momentum be gained,
through building healthy roots at home-
which does more than help us sustain

A better life awaits those
that know to set their daily tone,
while realizing through sweet wisdom,
that they must first take care of home

This Moment

I know a time that's precious,
that most folks overlook-
I know a time that matters more,
than any in life's book

That time is called this moment,
the time we have at hand-
a time folks take for granted,
sometimes due to future plans

No better time than present time,
to make the most of life-
We only have this moment,
this moment in our sight

This existing heartbeat-
This existing time;
We only have this moment,
this moment here to shine

Your Last Day

Today could be your last day-

You never really know,

so don't take life for granted

and let your self love show-

If there is something that you want

or feel the need to do-

today could be your last day,

so do those things for you-

Yes! put those plans to work,

and things you put off in the past-

Tomorrow's aren't forever

and today could be your last

Printed in the United States
By Bookmasters